Little Human Accidents

Chaos Poems from the Brink

Damon Ferrell Marbut

BareBackPress

BareBackPress

BareBackPress
Hamilton, Ontario, Canada
For enquires visit www.barebackpress.com
Contact BareBackPress at press@barebacklit.com
Visit the author at www.damonferrellmarbut.com
Cover layout and design by Choi Yunnam © 2013

Also by the Author

Awake in the Mad World

Poems

Little Human Accidents
Chaos Poems from the Brink

Damon Ferrell Marbut

Admitting Drunk to the Country

Friends know my process,
saddling up to the piano keyboard,
slamming my left wrist against a doorframe.

Mother said,
you're drunk.
I said,
yes,
but in italics.
And
you'll never know how revolutionary
everyone here thinks this is,
by a bridge somewhere
spitting syllables over the bricked side—
I think suicide wouldn't be horrible
if I died at the same time
in the river with the rest of the goats,
with the rest of everyone,
poets who apologize to me
when I get a little attention.

And true, poets are bad listeners,
don't know how to observe—

for the most part there is a handful
of moments where drinking
sorry white merlot, some kind of blush
rip-off, is the best sense-making thing
in a writer's world than having
scathing letters and pornographic pictures
sent to my home because I say,
yeah, you're terrible, but your business
is substantial in Polaroid.

We must remember all America is
is this poem, bad
breath and unaware,
sitting back on some drunk pill

like me that screams
at you how there ain't
no apology lurking like
a musical troll under the bridge,
I suppose the same one I mentioned earlier,
and hey here's Muriel again (you can't know)
getting me another beer when I've half a one
left. She writes like mad
while I get slurred and toilet-hover,
thinking hard on how this poem will fly
and about friends who still afford me
the freedom of telling it like it is —
they think stickin' it out with old Marbs
will bring a bit more good
than the things that get me
closer to drunk —

and drunk is bigger than any one of us —

I've lived eight-thousand,
seven-hundred-sixty moments of ugly or more
without excuses —

Muriel refuses to apologize
since she's said so much more than
this piss-poor society will remember,
I'll see everyone pro-this,
anti-that, let me step outside
and avoid the bugs like bullets
in a shit neighborhood of soon-to-be
ghetto hydrants and fuck-us-all
faggots like me, blowing smoke,
poem-ing at anyone who'll listen,
knees busted by asphalt and lunacy
screaming,
get your anti-anti
off my lawn!

And if it doesn't make sense it never will,
just spending time these days

waiting for Patrick to call,
singers to stop moaning,
a break in this shitty,
shitty night to turn to Muriel
and say you hear those horns?
that's me and the wine, the beer,
those loose articles
cracked against a wet rock
and a knuckled pair of middle fingers,
watching the stars and my shit-faced
eyes, pasted gay against
Ginsberg's queer shoulder,
that long poem John said he'd read
if he didn't need to wash his hands
so many goddamn times.

Little Human Accidents

The nightmare keeps you up tonight,
again, one you have each time it storms.
My poetry scatters the floor
all the way to the kitchen,

like a free-spirit sex train blew through—
you leave them there for décor,
love the way my poems smell in the house,
but you can't sleep.

On guard for me,
are you? Since you found me
beneath the furniture in the hall,
screaming, comatose, not knowing you
were there? Defending me from that?

Don't.

I can turn the lamplight brighter
and read you Billy Collins,

you're so gentle,

leave the battling of nightmares to me.

Apology

I haven't done anything with these years
but stay awake.
Was told my soul was over 150
by a pale thirty-something
with greased black hair,
large eyes, and a lot of Know
in his forehead's center

and I thought, to myself for once,
how this physical tuft of fur,
water and putty is a car
I can't drive, like explaining myself
over salmon dishes and house wines,
wheels turning endless
with the millennia
and I'm just tired
violin strings playing sad songs.

I've been abducted by a bit of sorrow
I resist along with clockwork,
though I don't mind the vacation from Earth,
like a test run before real death gets here
and I can start living —

perhaps that's the thing I've not done since birth —

or maybe I forgot to leave the womb.

I wrote that before, too.

I suppose
at 150 years we're allowed to slip
as I've said and done in past decades,
when my mind was less attached to direction
of this vehicle or the hum of its engine,

saying the same things over and over again
as my heart beats itself to death for me

to do this life right the next go 'round,
but at a truthful twenty-four, I know much better
than to expect that, or anything.

Every Little Thing

I read my Mother poems
as she sits on the couch
with a crooked, concerned look.

I know she doesn't understand—
she asks why I say *fuck* so much,
drink so much,
don't cut my hair.

I show her my credit card
statements and my cousin,
home from the Carolinas, says,
wow, you drink your credit cards

as mom tells me to finish reading
my poem. Her movie is on pause.

She's a terrible audience
and a bit daft—
I guess I just like the sound
of poetry in my broken
cigarette throat.

Bottles of Our Own

A friend of mine,
we both enjoyed Bukowski
for quite some time.

She bought a collection
of his for me the day we started
our first revolution on the bay,
when we found our flag and everything.
I think it was Nikki G.
that said
every nation needs a flag.

I can't remember. I was high on mosquitoes
and my notepad.

We'll call my lady
Courtney —
her name
cannot be
Courtney was concerned
about my poems, as I was,
and she wrote about me
pacing the shoreline and squawking
at pelicans, taking
breaks to read her Charles,
but not that one about empties
Adrien said was about us,

because we've gone through many
fulls, me and C, so yes,
a lot of empties, too.
But we've never been Charles
or that old car, never known
the dusty spit of making it back,
barely.

And Adrien,
I told her I was glad to have her around

17

and that she had more than potential
but talent,
intelligent enough to become good,
and that was before
Courts had gone out and scooped up the Chinaski book
with empties in it—

all his books say new poems
on it, the devil,
and we read it and laughed
at Courtney's smelly feet and said
yep, that's funny,
hilarious indeed.

Break from Academic

Early,
I'm tired of writing this conference paper,
trying to compare everything
to poetry, shit or sex.
Someone told me they all tie in
and I think yeah, like this could be
a shitty poem about sex, but it isn't—

It's convenient it is.

My friends and I are
a bunch of drunks
but we rarely complain
about making statements
the way ancient greeks did—
they don't get a capital "g" from me.

But they lived in the same kind
of time as us,
everyone hostile toward philosophy
like poetry today
because it meant something—
but where they went wrong
was in making everything so damned
unclear and wouldn't admit it.

Good thing Ginsberg wasn't around.

Can you believe
that poem he wrote?
Well *I'll be*, there it is,
one where he was barebacked
by some fella at a hotel
and he could smell feces while they
were on the job. Yeah, it all does tie in—
read Ginny's poem
for shitty sex,

but ignore the greeks
and me if you're smart.

Goddamn, can't understand how
this word processing gadget
thinks I should upgrade the "g."
I even write myself in lowercase
but not in a poem,
just in life—

always being right
is a huge responsibility,
which is why we're irresponsible,
me and my alcoholics
in the summer, arrogant
because we never sweat,
not in any kind of heat.

Cats Call

Hot inside. It's April,
cats complaining
from the utility room,
I think if Vinnie fell
again and meows enough
it means he's wedged
behind the water heater —
don't feel like walking in
to Sylvie staring at me,
paranoid, afraid I'll try
to pet her, afraid of Vinnie's
whining, he knows the drill,
lifts his paws so I can
reach under his belly,
slide him up the corner until
he can climb the rest
of the way. He needs
to do some work — helps him
feel less scared to get older —
good thing I've lost weight
else my arm would be too fat
to get him out, and Sylvie
would likely sit there,
lick her lazy crotch a bit,
study me with those frightened
eyes. We named her
after Sylvia Plath and I can always
seem to hear her thinking
Come on, Dad, do something.

Charles, Didn't You Know

We drove to a gas station
for smokes, lady friend had $1.94
in her account—
she's written to you.
We drove back, music was good,
searched almost five purses,
came up with enough money
for a pack, not two,
had to agree on the brand—
there were lots of pennies
nickels, dimes,
not too many quarters.
I said, *I love that we're poor*
and she felt temporarily pathetic—

I quelled that, quick.

We made our first cake
and I started a novel tonight
about second chances, I think,
and drinking champagne
before poetry readings.
The cake was so good,
supposed to be marbled—
ended up Marbut, instead,
and it was great, so tasty,
moist because of the extra egg,
if that makes sense.

That hard-earned pack of cigs
sits naked on the back deck table
as we write in separate rooms
and say, *let's write about this moment*
and then stop, go have a square,
read 'em out loud.

We used to talk in verse
and John would laugh at us

until he started, too.
He never ate one of our sandwiches
that cost less than three dollars to make,
that processed turkey,
like the unexpected cake
and cigarettes, like murder.

We talked about message,
if we'd like our lives to say
all those things our poems can't,
couldn't or didn't,
and we agree that we're finished with all this
stupid apologizing,
over-thinking, hoping hope
won't come back and bite us
in the ass, Charles,
to hell with you
and your dead whores
for making us stay up this early,
not worrying 'bout much anything
except how frustrated we are,
can't find that poem you wrote
that our friends say describes us —

you know I'm not mad,
nor is she, no energy around here
to keep pent up silliness inside
like anger, the bad kind.
We decide life at this point
is simply grabbing pennies,
other coins unstuck
in the car's drink holder
by drunk-spilled sodas,
decide that living right now
is the apology —
our last breaths, together,
the message.

Comida

Considering a burrito is a chore.

Mexican versus spaghetti,
no comparison.

I've showered: belly roars from beers
before breakfast,
cold vodka in the freezer —

I considered lots of things this afternoon
when the sun stayed home
and friends went down,
unshowered, perhaps ten times happier
than me, my skin,
smell of cologne on my head,
shampooed armpits,
soap-soaked nails
and, like saliva,
wet of mischief on my lips.

I'll choose burrito, leftover
from the restaurant where,
with two gone friends,
I lunched and swooned
at a boy not named Curtis
who brought tea, sweet tea
since we're in the South
I'd told him,

forgetting the pot of buh-sketti
in the fridge,

remembering the last time
I was alive in the a.m.,
thinking
on
drunk.

Psychology of Cool

It means a bit less than everything,
Muriel and me,
a different part of us both
connected by writing in the rain on a Sunday
where most all our poems originate,
like the last day of the weekend
is some kind of mother ship
and these fingertips are alien.
I can't get this quiet out of my skull
today, like maybe a vein will short circuit
in my hand and do something drastic
and wonderful to my heart—

Muriel's still asking if I'm all right,
and I realize my not answering
makes the two of us
a bit crazy. I heard her inner voice in a bar
once, a month back—
maybe I should answer.

But I can't shake off this dry sense of tired, too,
like there's a handful of poets on a street corner
in my head, flipping their hats
and asking me to read them some more
of that business on God and faggots—
my feet are hot in these shoes
but my knees hurt too bad
to bend and fix it,
keep drinking this beer Marbs,
there won't be knees
or Sunday poetry, which is fine,
need to find my car
and load it with throwaway words,
drive into a bunch of trees,
kill this silly energy

since nothing makes sense with the world
if people walk around thinking

it does, there's nothing in self
or faith, especially faith,
the way I thumb this goddamn
computer, too tired to masturbate
and unfortunately,
too alive to die.

Deadline

I tried to work on an essay
about Polanski's *Repulsion,*
lost a poem for good,
the one I wrote about watching Roman,

so now I write about writing
him,   even re-read the poem
this is all covered by,
thought of Muriel skimming it—
she told me she cried,
makes me want to cry today
while still drinking our cheap cola
since my teeth haven't rotted yet,
don't think they will.

And Johnny is so good today,
can imagine him bouncing campus
around on shoulders
of catharsis, he's really getting good,
you should read his work,
he trusts me when I tell him.

In my head we're all
listening to a different Davis
this afternoon, not Miles,
like I've said of Joni,
Alana has been miles, too—
can't shake how I feel so elated
today, like last night Mike
calling to say *hold on, brother,*
gonna make things great
for everyone.
He knows I've been roughing it,
think he may have said he loved me,
hung up before it processed,
wish I'd have repeated that
into the receiver—he knows though,
his wife is beautiful,

let's me tell her husband
I love him. Truly good,
this feeling of wholeness,
kind of wish a plane
would crash the roof of my home,
take me now
while the smiling's great.
Mother has funeral insurance on me
and my friends wouldn't be so selfish
to want me back, jealous perhaps
that I got a head start on living
past this physical world.

I talked to Steve in Colorado,
had given up on him
until today, gonna go ahead
say I love him, too —
lots of people worth loving,
sending that esteem into the world
is empowerment (another
curious goodness)
random poets about this town
dipping inquisitive fingers
into our well,
wonder why we cry all day
these delirious joy tears.

How it works is:
Yerbs writes responses to Muriel,
who responds to me
and John retorts,
all saving ourselves
from the wrong obscurities —
Dennis is joining this non-revolution,
saw him scream down
a stream poem the other day.
He's winning awards,
probably writes his essays on time
without squandering his life
with women on albums chanting

one day, yeah, some day, yeah
I think he does,
he hides it better than me —
go Dennis, you're all right
by me,

and this seems to be working,
two phones on my desk
in case Steve calls

he has a show tonight in Colorado
plays trumpet in a band
so
may I love him *now*?

And may I love Muriel?

She's on her way
from that damned French proficiency,
which I'm sure will go fine,
still picturing her tearing up
when she read
last night's release,
probably cried
because she knew I was unhappy
with the strange day
that led to the computer,
cold,
gray clouds out
confirming that silly rhyme
about April showers,
May flowers,

so here I go
off to Polanski.

Woke Before Dawn

Yes, Cam, I've had the dream
of skyscraper sway,
used it in conversation two days ago,
and I like that you know
without asking. I've been gone these days,
like a cat Kerouac would talk about
hitching with in the wind,
telling stories, and I can't promise
a return either, Cam —
found the edge I was looking for
so now it's jump or teeter,
but karma hasn't given me any options
other than a Doors record
and coffee as I mull the fall,

which won't be to the floor this time,
can't rescue my breaths from Sexton
when we drink beer next to grandmotherly
carports,
I have to *really* drop
there so I can hear your voice behind
my sand-kicking shoes,
can taste the dust trickle
like window rain and thoughts of honey —

I think it so true, again,
about no one understanding
my sandals beating the neighborhood
for answers, legs afraid of every step
over colonies of vulnerability,
lines of thoraxes under foot,

and as for my sheets, Cam, I sweat out
what my gnarled hands can't ever say
on paper — thank you for earlier,
thanks for mentioning angels.

Economy

America smokes cigarettes in white-knit
parking lots and dark pants —
I think the mustache man at fast food today
embodied that, walked from the grocery store
and seemed unhappy —
America smokes unhappy.

That teenage boy behind the counter
had a cut on his lip
and I told Muriel he'd probably been in a fight,
with fists, in the past eight days —
he had freckled arms, like her cheeks,
I thought about trout a moment
but didn't say anything —
being speckled on a Saturday ain't so bad
like the girl we named Katie
who yelled at him from her register
about something country,
something dumb enough
to know it was America
with a cigarette in its car-parked mouth.

Katie's mother sat rubbing her temples
over a tray of fat, not as fat as mine
and Muriel's, who said she couldn't eat
another bite

and
I turned to give shopping mall directions
to an out-of-towner who said thank you —
I said, sure no problem,
as though I had helped
and not sat with my back to her,
choking back freedom fries
and laughing at the stupidity of it all —
John says that's a bit of my inner asshole
and it probably is,
this afternoon says so,

like Katie's mom who was there to pick her up
after conflict resolution
between Katie and Trout—
all the customers heard everything
and Muriel said *no way.*

America is still smoking for Easter Sunday
and war that lasted long enough to call
a weekend a weekend, like a spade—
never was much for cards or killing,
I do that plenty on my own
like the fast food manager
who gave Muriel and me brand new cups
instead of refills, we said,
wow that's nice
and he looked at the floor.

It may be why those damn foolish
high school shits argued over where the packs
of ranch go, who will restock the condiment table,
poor Katie-mom, mosquito-bitten
thighs and varicose ankles,
I would have bought her a burger
if she wasn't ready to hit the pavement,
smoke with the rest of America,
Katie bitching in shotgun
about Trout all the way down
dirt roads they may
or may not call home.

Elegy for Florence

Mother brought home
Grandma's shampoo.
It sits around my bottles
and I can't, haven't yet touched them.

Patrick tells me I should.
He is right.

My cousins and I called her Nannie,
she's been dead for months
and her breath still envelops
my memory of her,
how she read silly gossip rags
and watched soaps,
switched me once for aggravating
neighborhood children.
I miss her placid laugh.
Don't know if I miss her.

I can't use her shampoo.

She had an ironing board in her bathroom
and Grandpa is broken
over her. They were quite a pair,
brought food to poor families
in their county, I tried to help
with money after my father passed —
it wasn't enough —
didn't help the way I'd wished.

Wanted to buy my Florence back.

Thought about this in the shower
after work, something that always
kept me from visiting (work),
a shallow excuse,
just trying to say "I love you"
now when now has quietly

passed and all there is left
is apple essence of Nannie
and her near
as I bathe,
like when I was a boy.

Faggot

His name is David in my mind.

I saw him lift that fag rag from the shelf
and hurriedly shove it back as we passed.

If David would have thought to ask
    we'd have stood around and kept watch,
let him enjoy wearing his green shirt
instead of those eyes frightened yellow.

He was with friends for whom I have no names —
they all had white legs, I guessed them servicemen,
thought against it since the war wasn't quite over,
    none of the three had muscular calves
so pasty   no muscle   one was hairy —
all made for a disappointing stalk in the bookstore
with my lesbian-in-training —
    she thought one cute and I agreed
as I picked up the nearest sexy shirtless cover,

glared at David and the macho letters
on back of his t-shirt. I wore one that said
something appropriately inappropriate
about white people, wondered if all the young men
together were one cohesive unit
of bitches who stitched at night in the closet.
    I told my quasi-dyke to help me find the lubrication ads —
she laughed aloud and David, well,
    we blew his

Five Dollar Poet

Today I hear a faint
clarinet, tea cups
hitting bottoms of soapy sinks,
my neck's strain to hear
the blue-tipped bead
of pen on my notebook.
I resist imagining how many elbows
have graced this counter,
have looked out despairingly
on a Tuesday and dreamed
or frustrated,
lost or captivated —
perhaps none of these.

Waiting for Isabelle
to approach from behind
and join me — her hand
is playful, warm —

I've been having
tense hallucinations of late,
hard to determine
reality from REM uncertainties,
and at least I know
she won't try to quell them —
that's the kind of good
I desire today.

Thought about ending the poem
but my hair is shaggy,
two-day beard sporadic,
unsure if I'm writing this at all
so *go on* I feel myself whisper —
haven't had a coffee yet,
been carrying these last five dollars
around, may not have anything
to drink

and then curiosity comes,
yes like a lover,
and I wonder how many
unheard blue-or-black-tips
etched soundlessly today
or any other Tuesday
when a few singles
in a left pocket
made so much the difference,

She knows
being poor takes courage—
my car's fed better,
rightly, it takes me
where I wish to go so I can
have good talks
about elbow-countered rain days,
cost of dying one line per moment,
searching coffee shop parking lots
over storm puddle glimmers,
fingers in my thick
high school boy hair,
smiling anyway.

The Boys Muriel and Johnny Fuck

I've never met,
but we agreed in the car last night,
somewhere on a highway between trouble
and perfection, that we've all had sex,
fucked each other at some point or another,
laying someone who nailed someone
who hammered someone from behind
and then kissed someone
who then turned and kissed
one of us, then we kiss each other —

so when Muriel says fuck
it's nineteen year-old boys,
so boys ain't a lie
but she's bedded a few men,
said she loved sucking Jim's penis
in Paris, they stayed in bed for days

and when Johnny says fuck
he talks about little cuddling bodies
and huge dicks, how he thought
what am I supposed to do with that thing?
a hundred times, or sitting with Neruda
and loving his simple ways to write
"I love you" into the tops of heads
Johnny pushes into his crotch

any lucky day of the week

I may never meet the boys they fuck —
it's so good to just say fuck —
I got one out at a poetry reading,
room filled with supposed conservatives
who said they were cool enough
for Ginsberg so I said, here comes the fuck,

and Johnny told me in the parking lot,
fuck you, let's go have a beer

and talk about orgasms again,
but let's not get in a wreck and die
like we did the last time we read poetry
in the car, drove tired from over the bay.

Last night we rode in the opposite
direction and I asked Muriel
where we were going, she said
Fairhope,
I asked
what's there,
she said
don't know, but between here and there
is a ton of road to drink on,
and Johnny laughed,
I said right on like I was from Cali
and thought a poem would
come out of all of it—
Johnny wrote three
but didn't mention
his face in a crotch or hands in pants,
maybe Muriel's, maybe mine,
I told you we've all fucked,

and Muriel's last talk of getting off
was in a poem that didn't
say much other than finding
the right way to go down
on that girl in her small blue car
that acts as a muse for all three
of us, digging that music
I told them both reminded me
of the crazy stuff I thought I saw
the time I ate acid too early in a shift
when I worked fast food,

and I've been careful not to mention myself—
they thought I'd write a poem
and confess, but the joke's on them,
expose   expose   expose

lesbo M and John,
she used to fuck guys
and I never
considered if Johnny has ever eaten
out a girl, but I can imagine his face
if I stay *stanks, don't it?*
and lean in real close,
tell him it tastes like old people's
bathwater and cat litter--

Muriel says no it doesn't,
she's eaten lots of it,
says she can suck a mean dick,
I think,   what other kind is there?
and Johnny never mentioned his technique
while he dirties his knees
for gratification, which is all blow jobs
are, a way to get an *attaboy,*

and I do hope Mike thinks this is funny,
he asked me last night to write
something witty so I did,
a poem about a gnat and I thought
it fairly humorous, read it to Muriel
(at work, cut her hand,
bleeding, bitching, I called her sweetie
and said, Aww, Jugs, I'm sorry)—

her tits are large, may hurt her back,
Johnny's got a prominent belly
and my ego's too big for one head,
so I guess it's time to do what it is
I do, start slamming this fucking poem
the way Yerbs does it,
stick-shifting around the city
saying fuck you, Mobile,
and your pretty little heterosexuals, too—
this poem needs a few more fucks,
like America, who has bad sex
on Zoloft,

I'm wasting time,
expose   expose   expose

myself

THE BOYS I FUCK
have all had huge cocks,
some liked tight grips
during hand jobs
and I have a small mouth and little teeth
so it is *difficult* to suck a dick
with the wrong equipment—
once tried to fuck a boy with
a sandwich bag for protection,
but I was seventeen, which is like
saying I'm sorry, I was drunk
or that I was in a fraternity —

the boys I fuck are scared
of me in every imaginable way,
they linger at my work places,
call me late at night
afraid I'll say no,

I *always* say no

Muriel and Johnny can tell you
that if I'm feeling nice
or have found a virgin
looking for an experienced tumble
I'll light scented candles
and play that opera album
Muriel hates but all real
fags enjoy, flip the guy's
legs in the air and make him
jerk himself
as I grunt and thrust
just long enough
to say *you can't stay here,*

I'll call you sometime

because I don't need to hear
"I love you" in the bedroom,
I like primal screaming,
sweating, hair-pulling
and if I shaved my head,
it wouldn't matter,
don't need *Oh that was great, baby*
in my ear, don't need a massage
and appreciation—like that boy
from Pensacola, thanked me
for letting him come over
and blow me in front of my roommate
like he'd won an award
I bestowed upon him,
I said you're welcome,
now go blow my roommate,
got a virgin coming over
in an hour—

the boys I fuck are usually beautiful,
basketball players, military men,
mall kiosk queens who sell sunglasses
(I fucking hate the word kiosk)
all boys as parts of me
though they don't know
Marbs,

how I love to study
the trees off Government Blvd.
on late mornings after a hard night's drink,
how I nervously overstep weeds
in my back yard while I read
Kafka I stole from a janitor,
his name was Carlito
and I wouldn't have fucked him
but he read good books,

or how I am unapologetic

and completely sorry
but not for the honesty
here, *you're* sorry if you haven't read
this far, scared like the boys
I fuck every time the doorbell
rings, they come to me
then I come, they go,
it's a process like anything else

and I hate that it's never a man
who turns my head,
never someone of substance
or better than being rough
as the poems that write me,
perhaps it's because I'm 24 and don't care much
for anything in love,
and someone might say
yeah, you're an asshole,
what do you expect?

but I don't expect anything, never have,
Muriel has a key ring that says that,
and until the day comes
when I disrobe from this outfit,
wear a different life that feels better,
I will say fuck do fuck eat fuck
live fuck until the boys are gone,
go fuck themselves.

Don't Need a Shirt to Come

I thought about how right she is
in knowing I run track up the street
to clear out noise—I get sound
instead, some poetic meal replacement
for my heart in early April spring.

My stomach isn't defined like in the past.
I love it, the way fatty skin
smothers muscle, still there,
hiding. I run without a shirt anyway,
past birds scuffling in brush
to the south, turn right
after a west-bound fifty yard jog,
face north and hear that same simple
scurry, wonder if the thrush
befriends the jay to confuse me.
I love their sounds, so natural and easy,
way I love my fuzzy,
kissable belly

and Johnny, he's lost it,
wrote two poems this morning:
one about loss of self,
other in regards to the ghost
of an orgasm. I once wrote *Orgasm*,
few jerked stanzas
by hand of an 18 year-old,
said nothing of sex,
captured only a whisper
of what I didn't know then,
and it burned like inverted match fire
crawling up the strike-anywhere
toward promiscuous typing fingers,
and that was when I handwrote everything,

and like a reasonable amount of climaxing,
"everything" could always wait

unlike Johnny, up at five a.m.
to write about Muse at his keyboard,
about vapor getting off
the free-spirit sex train
M digs so much
from that Collins homage poem
I wrote a month ago,
curious to know if Johnny washed his hands
before addressing his goes and comings.

I am out of breath and pacing
down the slope of cul-de-sac
where, again shirtless,
Jarod and Bryan used to play
modified versions of Homerun Derby
with me during summers,
we were in 8th grade,
our stomachs were smooth
while we were hitting tennis balls
up the street
since they usually rolled back down,
no need to give chase
until Bryan was at bat,

now he's fat and losing hair,
hasn't spoken to me in over 4 years,
he really is overweight and Jarod told me
in my bed when he slept over
how long his penis was, asked my length,
I lied about two numbers,
distance *and* how many times a day—
we sat atop a blue comforter
where I'd masturbated far more
than twice,
on the side where he'd have to sleep.

Good Son

The young granddaughter
of her friend from upstate calls her Ginga,

always asking me to write a poem about her,
and I do — it always misses —
I don't think she'll ever learn or catch on,
Ginga the Vomitous
Ginga the Bottle Tree Lady

Ginga, whose neighborhood children
aren't allowed by her house
after dusk,
she sneers,
Icky Ginga.

Ginga the Nosepicker,
index-fingering the universe,
reminding herself of her name
aloud in the hallway —
she calls me a machine sometimes
and I become cornfield Jenny
from Gump, wishing I could fly
far, far away from here —
Ginga the Soiled.

I used to think jazz would
pry her from the feeding trough
of existence like a strong hose
on two humping dogs — it is on a Thursday
that the real tragedy of her in purple
is sung, Ginga the Homophobe,
slinging queer around the cul-de-sac,
littered with pot-smoked chips
and a sincere fear of hemorrhoids,
which she's had and says they're tough —
now isn't that flaming?

She looks like a bunny when she eats,

a crazy one, I hope she likes this poem
but if not I'm sure I'll write more and more,
they'll get worse and worse until one day
the most horrible piece of trash I've created
will plop down on the couch next to her,
with television blaring,
and she'll say *son, this is beautiful*
this is your best stuff now scootch to the left
my program is on I'm drinking coffee
you smell like cigarettes don't forget your poem
I can't show it to the family it says queer in it
how can you say queer about me I don't really
like it that much (burp) I just don't I like Grisham
and that kind of writing you know
real writing —

I'll look down, like always,
get close enough to hate
before detouring to surrender,
think Ginga the Clueless
Ginga the Simpleton
Ginga the Jackass
Ginga the Manic
Ginga the All Mine
Ginga the Frightful
Ginga the Ruined
Ginga the Television Show No One Watches
Ginga the Terror
Ginga Sad Ginga —

and say, thanks Ma,

thanks for that.

One Long Stanza

Thought yesterday how I've never
written a poem about Craig,
lack of closure
and how the sex wasn't really as good
like if he were a full-blown fag—
he's in Tampa now,
scared shitless of this poem,
probably dating girls
when no one's watching,
it's truly sad, that boy
was quite beautiful
and I convinced myself
we were in love
for two years,
before I shaved my head this week
and stopped working out—
Craig always thought weights
were the key to sexuality
and I say nah, this keyboard
gets me in better ways—
he never listened when I
would say I write,
just dropped his shorts
and asked me to stick
it where the sun don't shine,
though nothing ever shined on Craig—
I hope he enjoys his tits
and fat paychecks,
I'll take my repugnance
to a bar, regret words,
sweat out the monkey
and remember
the last time I was on all fours
saying fuck me so desperately
like it was love—
he groped my crotch
the last time he was
in Mobile, I told him I loved him

but that he was an asshole
and he pulled away,
probably figured if he couldn't
have me then, ain't no use in trying
to get me back into those lotion
bottles, athletic supporters
when my body was great
and we both shaved everything—
Muriel says this poem is honest
and slays her, rather,
she used to say it,
now she sits back
and I tell her
sweetie, it's just
one long stanza,
hundreds of words too many
for this kid
who once had a twinkle
in his gorgeous blue eyes,
and then realized, shit Marbs,
that's all there is in him,
a brief spark that'll fizzle
the minute his dick goes
back in those Calvin Kleins
he tries so hard
to show everyone,
and they all knew he was gay,
just kinda waited around
for him to know, secretly
crying for me since they thought
the only damn thing
on sale at the Craig Store
was denial and fear
and I sifted through my pockets,
having just enough money
for rejection so I bought
that instead, pawned it
so I could buy this poem
and daydream on a Tuesday
as hammers hit the house

like ornery squirrels
plopping from the rain-soaked sky,
thinking about those girls
in Tampa, Craig
pinching his nose
and going down, lying about
the experience of his tongue,
proving to himself
and his three knowing
brothers that sure,
pussy can taste a whole lifetime of good.

Handwritten Letter

Again I find it Sunday,
stomach lined with cake
three times rolled with chocolate,
stood around a man
    whose wife glowed across candles
as four children chased puppies
and each other around the sausage grill
and a new vacuum in the carport,
    felt out of place, out of sorts, out of myself

                just felt out
and dirty for eating their cake
    though I'd been invited —
hands shook mine, kisses settled on my cheeks,
hugs everywhere

    I was sad
thinking about my poems —

my voice has become garbled
and strained — I'd like it back —
didn't use it to explain
what I'd inscribed on the inside
when the smiling father
opened my card,

it feels good to know what sad means,
how it trains the eye to spot glory
and love, worrying about Muse
tone
perception
love

and the rest can all wait for tomorrow —

it has to.

Written with a Hangover

There's a gnat
on the screen,
cool,
he just walked across the word gnat
and now he's relaxing above *screen*,
he just fell,
too far down the page
for me to type fast enough to get to him
and let him walk on my letters,
only an inch away, this is fun,
gnat writing, he's on the *ing*,
the one   above that space
now that *inch* an inch away,
it's wild like a board game,
gnat just crossed *and now* up there
we'll call him Payton,
Payton the Gnat, the new Stuart Little,
he just fell again,
I'd help him up to the ABC
button but would feel like that clichéd
Jesus reference about footprints,
shit,
I wrote about Christ and he ran away,
nope just on the screen's frame,
looking down at me,
Payton where you going
you so crazy
my poem ain't that bad
it's all about you
when it's not about me
getting low on ideas.

Honest and

barefoot,
I come back to the computer —
the sound of Velcro fly
ripping from my crotch
is the new soundtrack for tonight
along with M telling the back of my head
about her brother's sex life —
I pissed on her grandmother's
garden grate and some sand.
I wanted to go in a poinsettia pot
but didn't,
and there M sits arguing
with her laptop,
crazy ideas for poetry
and I say write it,
write on and I wiggle my toes
how she does when drunk.

Johnny asked her if she kicked
in the womb,
or just curled her toes
and she wasn't sure —
I'm certain I kicked hell
out of Mom,
said *let me out,*
can't raise hell in here.

Mom is a constant reminder.

Mom is constant, anyway,
consistent and wild,
silly and apologetic
like my ugly brown dog,
but Mom can't catch squirrels
like my mutt,
would be an odd sort of moment
to see the owner of the vagina
from which I was spat

with a dead creature
dangling from her hunting jowls,
kind of funny if you think insane
is the best way to feel American.

I wrote about weird America,
dwarf America and now I'm drunk —
this cigarette parted me
like Moses and the sea,
M's lips liked the wine taste
on the filter —
she's probably glad I didn't piss
her poinsettias,
glad I heard her brother-brothel
story, her voice resonating
a bit of mindless distance
between us, an impersonation
of a young man I barely,
rarely know, who sexes about
like most of my poet friends

and she said GO

just like that in italics,
write a poem it's late
and so beautiful-crazy-early,
I'll help you beat this thing out
tomorrow,

she still glows from Anne's
nice letter, called us all wonderful,
we don't need validation,
we're just content, happy,
aware that finally
in the middle of this un-poetic town,
there's at least a handful of people
who look around, smell the grass,
lick the stars like candy and wish
to be sitting on one of our couches
or deck chairs,

hearing the stellar sound of urine
lapping this goddamn Southern soil
like waves.

Hope You Don't

You bent open the front cover
of that poetry book, the anthology
Billy edited, to the point
I feared some bookstore clerk
would walk the aisles, condemn,
snatch it away,
and I had robot plans
of following her to the shelf,
grab another copy,
run straight circles until she tired
from the chase

since

she knew we had no plans
to buy —
I didn't tell you not to bend the poems,
you were
worried about Illinois, although I'd had
an Illinois vibe of late,
confused to find it was wrong,
afraid to sound like I sound
when asking you to write
about pickles, spears we bit
together, eyes closed,
feeding one another across the table
at lunch — old people thought us strange,
you poked me in the neck
so I guess you weren't cheating
after all,
our giggling was fun,
that cute blonde
(remember, I told her she was) may have thought us
strange, too, you gave her a nice tip
in terms of industry,
not just someone who thinks
a dollar cuts the mustard (you'd laugh,
I suppose, me with knife, mustard).

See how you're the second person today (?),
which doesn't make me so necessarily first
but if you called me that, I'd agree,
acting like a jerk's more fun
than being one and thanks, as well,
for lunch   too nice   to hear Izzy tell me
in one breath how she never thought
I hung over and how beautiful the South
is in March — it's almost April, rain,
warm enough to play in it
in goofy t-shirts (your breasts are big)
you should wear a tight one.

I hope you don't think this silly,
your being the "you" of this poem —
we rode here together, I'd hate to walk home
in sandals and miss dinner with Johnny
wherever we are going to eat,
since he might read this, say we're crazy —

well John?

In and Out   of

One shoe on,   one off,
began to write a poem but had to up
and go to the bathroom for a bandage
after I picked loose skin from a reopened
wound — didn't think of all
the metaphors for that until typing this stanza.
    See I'm exhausted — writing poems
and dancing near bay water takes out everything,
like breathing azalea air mixed with wisteria,
    purple and pink tangible perfumes can last
in the heart even if it isn't daily, though   it should be.
    That's what I'm supposed to feel.   I think
a deep red blood drop would help me understand
my life.

Shoes off,   blood clotting,
    can't use my middle finger still   though
I doubt it's needed much beyond this   to say the least.
My shoes are so good,   sitting patient
and floppy by my side —
    I can slip in and out of them now   when before
    as a kid   I thought it'd ruin the heels.
    Guess my mother was telling another story
about how to manage things I worked so hard for,
    or maybe *she* worked hard   and I was in a trance
to think they were really mine,   like this poem
I happened to cripple down isn't really mine anymore,
    just ramble mind scramble,   a different way
I can talk about why I'm so very tired but can never
                                        fall asleep.

On an Index Card

Kind of let down at 1:34 in the morning
wondering what Patrick sees in my poems,
ruffled and facedown by his couch
and if the smell of bacon he cooked
when I was drunk still roams the condo
like a ghost inside the city.
I hope he's not running,
hope he doesn't crave escape —

he lives behind an Irish pub I've closed down
before, once saw a bartender throw up
in the trash because he did too much cocaine —
Patrick gets stoned — I'm confused
on Isabelle's porch with a pirate flag —
spitting to my right, exhaling smoke to my left,
noiseless schoolyard across the street
with no passing cars, a hint of neighbor laughter,
crickets,
like the night isn't supposed to include me
in his arms as I write poetry in the living room,
his eyes at my face that struggles
to get the words right the first time —

he doesn't know I'm an odd perfectionist,
unaware how I read him the day we met
and still needed him around, like now,
crazy to anticipate the phone's ring
and know it's him before the receiver touches
the same ear he tongues because it drives me wild

like running out of cigarettes and trust for people
who say I miss you and my first name
in the same sentence,

who pick me up
when I cause myself to stumble,
too good at this game now to say it's
just the booze —

I can take a yes, handle a no,
had plenty of both but nothing so sweet
as him in the kitchen, bare feet
and boxer shorts only,
saying *I know you're hungry, baby,*
your poems are so good.

Something for Insensitive

Should have left the bar last night.

Isabelle said something about her cat
with worried eyes — think I heard
that it was caught and dragged
under a car tire for a block.

I should have left the goddamn bar to see
and it didn't register.
I kept nodding
and nodding, as drunks do.

She loves her animals more than
her boyfriend, though he's a wonderful guy
who plays bass and likes Dylan,
dogs and Isabelle's cat.

Would have left the bar last night.
My mind said something about Patrick
with a sated smile, which held me there —
I called him at work, twice, told a friend
in New York how I do that at times,
leaving out that part where I abandon
upset friends for dollar PBR.

It doesn't matter,
I kept saying and saying, as liars do —
Isabelle couldn't have used what little help
I'd have given.
Perhaps I'd have tucked away
in her Volvo's back seat,
cigarette burned down to the filter,
snoring as she cried on a neighbor's shoulder —
Isabelle hates her neighbors —
would have been awful to wake
and see her uncomfortably held
because I was too drunk
to stand, like a man, and do it myself.

I wish I'd gone.

This morning I got home
from a lover's house,
studied our new refrigerator,
thought of new things we'd soon hang
or stick on the polished face
of the freezer, let out my cats:
Vinnie followed me into the bathroom
as I sat and read Meagan's poems.
I called her and said two were good,
two belonged beneath me.
Her message beeped time's up.
I wiped and stood. Vinnie pawed me
on the leg.

He's an old cat, probably fifteen,
got him to replace Connie
when I was a little boy,
may have cried like Isabelle,
can't remember that far back
but I bet Vinnie can
and suddenly I find
it's painful to muster that image,
old loyal Vinnie ensnared by tire tread,
hard to acknowledge how one day
I'll walk around the house,
make those soft lip-kissing sounds
he likes so much, not see him
loyally trot the entertainment system's corner
and meow with those green eyes,
tail straight up to the sky.

I wonder if scenarios went down like that
in Isabelle's head as she drove home,
if she could see blood on the pavement,
mauled cat expression like a photograph
pressed to her forehead as I stood
in the center of that uninteresting bar

filled with semi-interesting people —

if friends start calling me Ol' Marbs
without smiles or playful breath
I'll begin to worry about myself
and how I drank that cheap beer,
passed out on the lounge couch
with my face toward the ceiling
like Vinnie's tail,
mouth widely agape,
terrible and sad like the cat
that no longer belongs to Isabelle.

Excuses for Insomnia

Started wondering how I sit
and spit out all these poems,
or *pomes*, depending.

Can't say I like them all —

there are those horns
in the background,

kind of smooth now

and I feel old
like Sam-who-looks-like-a-Ben
could pop up from nowhere
and say *you're twenty-four,
shouldn't you be in bed?*

if he did I'd probably
tell him drinkers don't have to have a bottle
nearby to act like a drinker,
tip my hat,
ignore his fussing over serious
editing, done too much,
like I will this,
line it with frustration marks
and bleed it black,

can't use Muriel's green,

she's writing about me
somewhere across town
at a desk where best edits
muscle best-ed poems,

again,
pomes, all they really are,

and Jack knew,

wrote rambling poetic belches,
felt good because he knew the time,
can't have it now, or ever,
can't do much but nothing special these days

except poets misspelling "except"
the first go 'round,
not catching it the second,
waiting for drunken lovers to call
so we can say *love you, too*
before hanging up,
realizing Sam-Ben was right,
we should *all* be in bed.

Itinerary

So she said 4:30 a.m. was her best time —
we all laughed and said
that's about when we go to sleep

like right now,

and I wondered for a bit more than a second
if she was a closet drunk,
sat up sipping box wine
and playing thumb war with all those
characters she writes about,
pulls her hair and reads Donald
or James or Miller for a hint,
clue,

something better than a refill,

if she hums songs in her head
along with Armstrong or Sinatra
or writes in silence,
spins in her chair when the right set
of words hits the paper
like spit from someone's
excited speech.

Thought real hard against it,
old finicky twitch in the middle
of my forehead again,
been banging this machine to death
all night and now it's morning —

I kick myself constantly
at least *knowing* I should sleep —

got a friend here somewhere
around the house slapping laptop
about an uncomfortable girl
with some jerk she likes but doesn't love —

I think so quiet
I can hardly breathe
how she can
sit there with new pains
in her back, like my usual ones,
beat hell out of anybody
but herself for sitting in the dark
and jerking off her brain
before sunrise.

Poem for John

She sleeps, John —
that French thing is tomorrow —
she's written so hard, like you
she keeps me awake.

I see a computer screen glow
bouncing your tears
like children's *Star Wars* sabers,
eyes darting the room
in which you sleep,
and I've never been inside 'til now,

I see you crying Johnny —
didn't you read my poem
about battling nightmares?
I can't rescue you,
don't wish to try,
knowing you can rescue yourself
in every line you growl
and curse and laugh
onto the screen or into a notebook
buried in your lap,
leaping from your chair

(I know you do)

when the right word falls like heavy snowflakes
into your   hair   it   isn't disgusting,
nothing about you is,
we've talked about spears-in-sides,
both lived it a time or two,
wish I could rest the way you are,
where you are, how you are
in a cocoon of gladness,
where melancholy transforms
into beautiful verse —
your wings are so alive,
can't you see them, John?

Come, just this once more
(you know I'm big into second
chances, they help me heal),
give me those garish thoughts,
have one of my hearts
to do what you will,
use it as parchment for poems,
write down more of this wonderful
life you have become.

Lagniappe

Jim would say not to write this
but it's fiction, really, like John
saying he wouldn't tuck anyone in last night.
He did, it was Muriel and me,
cooked us eggs and bacon good,
boxed pancakes bad, but we still ate —
I called those flapjacks gross
and someone said *thanks for that*
before I landed on the floor and slept.

Muriel threw up on her hands,
too drunk to lament her inability to type
without making a mess,
when all poetry does is spread ideas about
like dumpster litter,
and I guess who picks us up for a good read
is the garbage man. If they set us down,
they can't understand or don't want to,
and Jim, I had a bit to say after lunch
with Muriel at a sandwich bar,
guessing peoples' lives through windows
like I've done before, and that was fiction,
you prick, that was fiction
for real.

Love Like Me

Every town has a boulevard,
an MLK Drive, too.
I drive the boulevard at 2 a.m.

Street side lights saddle the four-lane —
I think of many times in high school
when my eyes, confused by LSD,
misinterpreted the dull glow
for Thompson clarity.

In high school I killed a hamster
after a midterm. Vick saw it slide
down the classroom wall —
I didn't mean to shake it off my finger so hard.

On the boulevard, driving home
I regret that hamster. The story gets told now,
8 years later, and I wish that goddamn rodent
wouldn't have bitten.

There's an attractive blond boy
in a beat-up blue Toyota on my right,
taps his fingers to the same beats —
I wonder if he listens to my song.
He studies me, speeds up, resisting temptation
or anything else. I don't think to catch him,
can't afford to waste the gas,
realized him an old schoolmate anyway,
was a quiet boy, perhaps that explains
the attraction.

Wrote notes for this poem on back
of a job application, can't turn it in now,
pressed stapled papers against the horn symbol
of my Jeep — on the radio Natalie sang how night
belongs to lovers; I think, *what* lovers?

Then I remember one of our bar regulars,

Kevin-something, came in tonight and told Lynn
he'd had a relative die on him the previous week,
sounded like brother, or mother. I wondered which
he'd need to lose to not go to a bar
and talk about it. Kevin-something calls salmon
sall-mun, probably treads unsafe boulevards
every night, might resist the same things
as the blond Toyota boy, may fear discussing cuisine
in a bar over dead family.
Perhaps not.

I pass a few stoplights,
wonder at the idea of writers' power.
Defeated poets argue how everything's been said
already. They are wrong. They talk too much.

We've strength in originality,
don't need to waste time worrying
about impact — over-analysis only weakens beauty.

I drive past Patrick's apartment,
wanted to see him but yearned to write this poem
before it fell from my car like loose change.
He called and said he'd hold me
while I worked it all out by pen, reminded me
of a younger Jim having Julie
rest in bed as he wrote; I wonder
if she truly rested. I u-turn at the next median.

Confused about my emotions now,
to think I'd say no to Patrick for a silly
piece of poem, afraid he'd kiss me less
with beer on my lips, cigarettes on my tongue.
He mentions odor of bar smoke
when he meets me at the door,
kisses me anyway,
cooks black beans and laments a lack of onion
for flavor. I love that he'd eat onion
without trepidation before touching his tongue
to mine. He has lazy, sleepy eyes and a wry,

sexy smile. I like that so much. John thinks
he is a keeper.

Patrick sings a line from my favorite song,
says he sounds like a pro —
I tell him otherwise — he playfully calls me mean.

We converse about the jouissance
of *Great Expectations,* me on his couch,
him in that real blue iridescence of the kitchen —
we say things about ourselves and agree
to disagree. I remember once more, Natalie
on the radio, me buried somewhere in tire-laden
boulevard streets, coming and going,
her voice still carrying on about lovers.

I revisit that mindless question,
what lovers?
and feel Patrick's fingers,
curious about my back

and think,   Oh yeah, that one.

Lunch Today

Sweating poems doesn't work —
sweating poetry does.

I wrote perfect once,
two women told me so--

it was so, I guess,

but lunch was good.
We spoke in verse
real quiet,
and our chicken fingers
were real, riblets
from Rachel having a bad day —
we gave her cigarettes,
asked her about sex.
She laughed.
I guess her day got better,

and then we *and*-ed more into the car,
ambled around in the afternoon sunshine
and Liz, our new friend,
spoke of me in third person,
liked my energy,
wanted more.

We let the radio take us home.

Mind Growl

A flash message beeped,
across the room, through a wall
as I tried to doze, blue light
(like in most poems) blazed
as though I'd hit an unseen button,
awakened some pocket-sized galaxy
tucked behind the ceramic jar
on my nightstand(s). I have two,
only one gets used — let's not personify
the other, it doesn't need attention,

but

the room was lazy-calm,
kind of good in determining
silence at perfect moments.
People should respect small space,
its ability to necessarily quiet,
how no one predicts Time's downward
swoop, like a mad hornet,
passing out chaos like candy
we swore we'd give up
and then forgot.

Mornings Like This

Holed up in my home office,
poetry collections by my feet,
scattered, and I'm wearing
shoes, would rather be barefoot
and digging toes into sand —
it doesn't have to be beach,
backyard dirt is just fine.

I bet it's hot out, like the couch
where I slept with a radio
on the floor pulled near my head.
I didn't sleep well,
sweating out beers and curiosities
of night, and the "she" of this poem
curled in her grandmother's bed
with a quiet fan working like mad
overhead,

I woke

thinking I was someone else
and tasted chocolate,
mucus, went to the bathroom
and spit,
joined her in the back,
lay beside her as she opened one eye
and said hello with that
dreamy appeal I get hard over,
and my tongue tasted like pot,
we smoked so little of it
but I'm a lightweight,
she said,
I added icing to a pastry
at three a.m. and drank her under
the table,
she often says
it's hard to keep up,

and today is Friday,
feels Tuesday, the house
is more quiet than it's been,
she was dismissed in love today
same way I was let go
in poetry —
guess we both have dark clouds
sometimes saying they
are the goddamn sun,
you hear me, Marbut?
I'm the fucking sun —

and there she goes
in the living room —

she kissed me, rather,
let me kiss her
and I hadn't yet brushed my teeth,
was thinking about a cigarette
and some of that pastry
or sandwiches, forgot about those,
ones we live off because feeling poor
kind of comes along with *being* it,
and I stepped on her copy
of Stafford's something-or-another
which I picked up, asked her about,
read two poems
and stuck the book
back under my shoe,
not in the mood,

's why we left that reading
last night over the bay,
drank beers in a pub
and watched people die in the dark,
may be why we almost died
driving ninety on the way home —
I was talking about orgasms
with a friend in the back seat
as my "she" drove —

I've died a hundred times
in uglier places than on that highway,
I told 'em, what's one more death,
might be the one that saves us,

but we all made it home,
    drank more beer
    laughed off our shakes
    read poems huddled
around this FBI agent
and his girlfriend, smoking
cigarettes and wondering what
they'd gotten into,
and I asked John to read Sexton,
the one he reads so well,
better even than Anne —
I probably only like *Her Kind*
because of John and the way
he says "ribs crack" —

I fall to the floor sometimes,
even when I'm not awake.

Number Nine

Heard this song,
got it going now, actually,
on repeat,
reminded me of riding in the car
with one of my sister's
high school boyfriends
on the way to Coach's house,
a beat up shanty-type dust hole,

and in the car he howled
lyrics toward the roof,
it was great and wild —
when we got to Coach's trailer
there were lots of cars everywhere,
I'm skipping around
by then,
I found a red ribbon
and gave it to a blonde,

got a testicle
caught in my zipper, not really,
lied to a different blonde
who leaned over,
said oh baby
are you okay? and gave me a menthol cigarette —
it was cheap and gross like the lie,

drank Schafer in a can
because I didn't know, some Evan
mixed with schnapps
which stung so bad I couldn't open
my eyes, I was thirteen, got another hug
from ribbon girl,

saw two cheerleaders dip snuff
and puke, they were twins,
come to think of it and there were
several guys pissing around a fire,

that's where Coach hung out,
near all the youthful cocks,
he said he liked to write and wanted me
to love him like a father,
to kiss him on the cheek
and asked me to call him Dad—
I think his mother had been murdered
in Louisiana,
he liked Bud Dry
and when everyone left the party
I was drunk and stayed over,

around 4 a.m.
I'd guess
is when he forced
me down on his lap
and hoped I was too drunk to remember,
his dick seemed big to a child
like me,
a kid I still see from time to time.

Mother doesn't know being bound
or how growing into me hasn't been bad—
this crybaby poetry lies around useless
and kinda like cigarette ash if you wanted
a simile there, were too polite to ask,
but the poems make me feel all right—

I was going to masturbate but wrote this
and lost my nerve, since that little boy's reading this
over my shoulder,
plus,
no matter how you look at it,
my heart's not in most anything,
nowhere near midnight,
I've not had coffee,
just hit the wrong button on the player,
now I may have to write a poem, number ten,
a poem per song—
I got time.

Inside My Nose

I used to think cocaine
was a joy, have a friend
who came out of his seat
when I said I'd once
been up for days at a time
on coke and crystal,
shouting at the world
as my nose sang along,
poor septum,
I'd get high and think
less than once how
that straw fit so nicely per hole,
sniff after snort
after back-of-throat inhale--

now I just pick it, my nose,
pinky most often used
but sometimes thumb,
and a girl friend laughs
because I forget where I am
and who is watching,
fingernails still remember
the nights I'd wake up
from zombie days,
scraping out leftovers
from a night with too many cigarettes,
a plate, few half-gallons
of vodka
and a couple of seemly men
who liked to hear me talk,
would do most anything
to keep me around
because I often
used to say yes.

Older Than Now

Since my hair has outgrown me
I play with it often,
wrinkle my nose in case someone
is watching, give them one last chance
to think me cute,
boyish,   before thirty gets here
and I have to start thinking about insurance,
let my face's expression lines
turn from a playful tan
to jaundiced academic has-been,
which may happen,
but I hope I'm too gone.

Haven't placed a straight razor against my cheek
in weeks.   Muriel says
fuck 'em in such an adorably mannish tone
I can only remark that her breasts are big,
come just short
of accurate about her cup size
and then my hands are dry, fingertips growing
right along with the hair,
stomach resisting my past soccer body —
I laughingly drink diet soda
and pause from poems
for cigarettes and reflection
in blue cars on bluer highways,
all the beauty the city can handle
jammed between an overflowing cache
of CDs and love letters,
poems and prose separating me and Muriel
most nights our animals waken
and drive us close to wild desire,
the hungriness David writes about
that M sits back and loves
so down
like a child
I would never be again
unless I rolled over in back pain

one morning and decided to recede,

and all my worries in the shower
down the hall were about Caley,
from where the mist of her face came
I can't know, perhaps it was
a scene of ballroom dance partners
and girl crushes versus boy defiance,
    she was this sickly blonde
in grade school who'd confessed
with trembling lower lip
to me, in back of art class,
to not turning her dad away
when he'd advanced a few months earlier
and not stopped until entering
little girl places, ignored the pure trust
of little girl hearts   as she shook —
I wouldn't know for months
that she had some awful disease,
would shake off so many pounds
she'd look like a prickly ghost
of death and wear leg braces
that Mom bought, dad put on
and took off. Caley knew
I didn't like her,
then I hated him
in a sort of selfish way
because I finally had to start knowing,
glad the rape of my youth
was different from hers,
and I held her hand
since holding hands
works in the dentist office

and she had certainly pulled a tooth.

Perhaps I thought about being saved,
which is why I thought of her
like the bottles of vodka
and cheap wines have lent me

blind expectation, that sometime soon
I'll find a boat that drags me around
the ocean of real,
or what I *think* is real,
just long enough for me to smell something
other than the scent of my face aging,
sound of bones popping and those talks
about bad knees and being unable
to run on treadmills,

and there again is Muriel,
fuck 'em, and I think

sure, worse shit happens
to better people than me.

Patella

Watched my legs this morning
walk around the house,
kind of tan like the walls,
and I'm sure my knees
are going out soon,
John says I have a throat chakra
or something like that,
but I feel knees —
he says my totems are hummingbird
and dolphin,
the first being masculine
like all that hair on my legs
over scars and hidden cartilage.
Muriel is panther and turtle —
we got it all sorted
over three and a half bottles of wine
one dinner, got high
and determined everything else.

Later I lay on the couch,
Muriel wrote a poem
and said Marbs,
you going to bed?
and I said sure I'll have pizza —
she told me there was none
so I shifted on the cushions,
said M,
I'm worried 'bout my knees,
but John don't know,
I got it all figured out.

I Don't Need a Poem to be Free

Little pink book,   its binding pouts
untouched onshelf, I said
I'd rather a vodka—Muriel laughed,
asked for paper,
didn't need a poem either.

Barefoot we sat splayed
in an afternoon bookstore,

I supposed something
could free me, maybe
the beautiful children
watching us read satiating Lehman,—
perhaps
they study our unfortunate Whitman,
how we agree "that doesn't sound him"—

I think of all that sperm
in the waves spattered by rain
that Nikki said was sperm from God—
so much ocean getting pregnant sounds
somehow very nice,
and it's difficult to write
in the children's section
around toys clicking toys by boys
and girls sitting in the big plastic Choo-Choo,
watching,

I'd guess no poem frees
or enslaves unless we let it,
blame it,
say it made us this way
or like these kids
making fighter jet gun noise
with spit-puckered lips.

I wish
they didn't live in a time of impressions

of fighter jets—
I wish they didn't know at all
and that the sound of guns fired into jungles
or cities sounded a lot like laughter.

Pull Over

I think police aren't so bad,
some just working out that kid dream
of saving people
like firemen or just appeasing
hail-of-bullets erections,

and others taking away drugs
to their homes—I know a few
trainees in the academy who said they
plan to yank pot and crack
from cars. It's cool, they say,
girlfriend will like what their salaries
can't provide and it will probably
help with sex

but I really think, now
in front of the computer,
after a nice neighborhood walk,
that policemen are a bit like the moon,
lurking somewhere in darkness,
just trying out their hand at saving
what's left of good in the world
though that's changed, too.

Perhaps I should keep this poem
behind my steering wheel
like a photograph of a daughter
to give a cop the next time
my drunk bumper tags a tree
or mailbox—might have to pluck weeds
again like after my first DUI,
the cop can say I saw you
flick that cigarette, want littering on here,
too? and I'll say read my poem,
I'm one of the ones who's *for* you,
and maybe he will let me
play with his badge
beneath a quiet night crescent.

I can ride in back
with no cuffs because I'm friendly,
I'll end up remembering those damn weeds,
really digging me when I was nineteen
and in jeans on my knees
not thinking nicely about the police —

the cop will say, hey Marbut,
your judgment ain't so clear
but I like your poems —
I'll smile with my teeth and take off
my shoelaces, he'll need them anyway
for the sleepover,
stretch my stomach for those dry,
gorgeous jail pancakes
and think damn,
where's that poem
for sending good vibes
to the wife beater,
the transvestite? and watch
the moon through
the cruiser window,
a shade more sober
than before.

Rolodex

I am sexually inclined
toward the fluidity of things,

and here is most of the past year,
resting on cold bare knees,
toilet shorts ankled, thinking
about direction, it's before dinner,
I play

with A, friends of lovers
I call or avoid, numbers I've taken
to know when not to answer,
businesses and then B, mainly out of-town
friends, Mother, favorite bookstore,
an old drinking companion,
then a snare of C, people and places
I wanted to make love to, or did,
before they faded
perhaps it was me

and D is lovers and co-workers
and father and teachers and a handsome boy,
now a professional golfer in Florida
he begged me to call and I didn't,
some have laughed, said I missed a good chance
but I didn't miss much,
I'd rather be responsible for my own opportunity,
one musician whose son is famous,

people I'd soon forget in E,
a couple I almost *did* until today,
no real F or G or H

one fabulous I,

troublesome J, lovers,
so many lovers, one I would take back
and undo, one who wanted me

desperately, I took his friend instead,
my way of saying *no*,
one who hates me for saying *no*,
two true friends
before arriving at L, an uncomfortable slew
of inconsequential women,
wanting and wanting,
a few good ones but I flip too quick,
some crazy feminine M and N,
a good lover

O P R all the same,
no one knows Q
winding me around corners
of silly memories, most pages
were torn from here
I assume I'd been drinking then

and

no chance in S,
a tragic T, a hopeful one,
a T who hired me, one who fired me,
two who *tried* to hire me,
two poets and no U,
never is,
one V and all her numbers,
a nearly forgotten W
who fell from his chair once,
a red-headed W from Atlanta,
drinking buddy Y
and a severe lack of Z
(somewhere doing shots with Q,
I would think)

but the categorical letters
ignored here are unwritten
chapters,
I hope to fill them soon
with more love

and less lovers,
   no longer the poet who thinks
sex should be an everyday occurrence,
or as random as before,

some friends would call me
cheap to buy another rolodex,
otherwise my phone would be unhooked,
avoiding the angry many who call

because I loved too much
or never loved at all.

Sarah's Eventual Poem

Make it last,
an odd voice whispered behind my head—
chilled vodka stood between
my newest poetry book and failure

and I reflect on Sarah
storming from the lounge
several Thursdays ago, back bumper sparking
a sloped exit (she never drives this way)
she sent messages, desperate pleas
for me to write about her
so now I do,
vodka has a warming sensation
and I'm wearing white—

smoked one of Collins' best cigarettes
this evening, early and dark
at the end of a wealthy poet's driveway,
her neighborhood trees generous
with the view of stars—
I could see them through my eyelids,
which was nice,

I'd had three drinks by then,
wondered at two airplanes,
tried deciding which one
to dream to, figured there must have been
some point in history when a passenger looked
at the right spot on the ground,
wrote a poem down to a poet
scribbling up—they probably argued in verse
over who had the better view,
perhaps held their gaze several states
and pages later.

Sure it's been done,
supposing at planes,
been told *I've* been done before,

and that most of who I am
doesn't matter, wrote about who said that, too,
she's *over*done, has been,
maybe jealous she never had someone
named Sarah driving mad on her behalf —
I think she's just angry
having never been invited
to sit at artists' homes,
smoke fresh smokes,
listen to me describe how those unimaginable
Southern stars
carry away north, west, east and how I can see
it all without peeking,
sometimes tug constellations down,
rest them in front yard trees —

it warms me
with the vodka
in ways it never will Sarah.

Shape-Shifter

Got a friend who turned into a wolf
somewhere in New York one night,
so many years ago —
I get distracted when he talks of Californian Buddhas.

Got a friend in the other room,
writes poems so furious
I think she needs an Indian name,
she yells how I'll die
when I hear her newest.
I probably will. I have before,

and we're sipping so much of this
ugly pink wine, it's cheap,
same brand my dead grandmother
drank and worried about becoming
an alcoholic at seventy-seven —
I pulled it off at twenty-four
so drink, Granny, drink,

but don't worry about consequences,
there are none on this keyboard,
none on these hands or under this lamplight,
I just wonder if my own silly wolf
will come back just long enough
to take care of me, tiny Kipling boy,
put his forty year-old paws
about my unassuming child head,

and scream,
grrr, goddamnit! grrr!

Solipsism

Don't know to believe in self anymore,
if I can verify anything
in philosophy,
or confirm Sartre's *Other*,
or feed at this desk
and still be hungry,
swallowed by want
or different one-word concepts
for failed admittances
that, even as poets,
no one knows a thing
except to avoid saying *Other*
when Jean-Paul's in the room.

Walked the neighborhood circle
before dusk, and when the light was gone
it was gone, read *Being and Nothingness*
and disagreed at the pages —
elderly couples passed by
with raised black socks,
single female jogger,
one family of four.
I thought perhaps they *couldn't*
see me,
maybe there *is* only me

and the last thought to fall out,
   splatter sidewalk
   beneath the fireflies
was that it is quite nice
to go a long, long way

aware of nothing,
unsure of it all.

So What

This is how it feels to live a poem—
Muriel heard me belt through the house
questions about Mike's karma, and I hate the telephone,
don't watch television,
don't care much for anything tele-.
Azaleas in the front yard kiss wisteria
and that big dogwood, reminding me
of the sign of the cross. Don't care much
for that, either.

We talk in metaphors,
agree we should,
we're just discovering
it's all right to make sense from nothing—
I had a few too many drinks last night
and didn't think it wrong, either, lots of eithers here
and no sense at all.

I love that I'm coughing—
we're having a life day and I can't breathe,
feels nice dripping into deathly feel
as I write new poems, she edits hers—
We just can't stop laughing.
Laughter is a curious goodness,
feels sexual when one isn't in mid-cough—
she called me Vlad and I said, *guilty,*
I have impaled,

and it wasn't funny,

but we live long lives of unfortunate near-misses,
letters from seductive hopefuls, men and women
wishing to learn to write
but afraid what they'll find, something like this,
an awareness of the beauty of outside
flowers, big bees or whatever they call themselves
these days,
and we're inside, me and my wonderful

Muriel creature, living She-on-Vlad,
almost out of champagne — we know a few bartenders
around town willing to open early this afternoon
for us to read them poems — we'll drive in a Dodge
and tailgate. I wish we'd have bought orange juice,
as we were feeling an OJ vibe at Granny's house —
I took a diet coke and didn't share.

But this is how it feels to live a poem,
with piano somewhere around the house,
apple sauce and cooked mettwurst in the fridge —
I'm glad I thought to write this
when cold champagne was here
and not some of mother's cheap blush.
She doesn't drink much,
I don't care for her much either
but I wouldn't trade her for the world,
having learned too many things
where she failed, succeeded in having me —

and I'm not a hunk, Muriel says so
as she pets the side of my face,
me, dreaming how nice it could be to call back Mike,
help him plant wisteria (I told him it would
be a *sexy* back yard)

          since I think living like a poem is sharp, and pretty,
my baby sits with me — I want to kiss her
neck because she likes it there,
afraid to talk about *suck* since everyone thinks dirty
things when *suck* is around,
nothing dirtier than my fingertips balancing this keyboard,
not saying anything more than how being alive,
writing poetry, having cocktails too early
to be having cocktails is an art — I hope someone reads
this when I'm gone and says,
imagine what it would be like
to have lived the way they did
and we sit back, knowing this might happen,
clink our glasses (mine is really a bud vase)

not worried about anything except going
to see beautiful Isabelle (Muriel and I agree she is)
and watch her fix us drinks,
thinking real hard about where the next poem will strike.

Specifics

Took off my sleeping pants
and changed shirts, so cold
in the house,
and this is how I dress,
socks still on,
unsure as to whether or not
heat escapes my body
through feet or head —
afraid to call it *my* body,
just a rental from the universe,

but I do feel a chill,
lips'll probably chap under the fan
this body's too lazy
to switch off,
and again,
scared to say *the* fan,
no more special than kinds
that whirl over-bed-head,
cooling prettier people
than yours truly,
ol' dirty socks,
neither foot
touching ground
(they haven't yet)

and once more, frightened
to be *yours*,
I've never done much truly —
friends know I run when pressured,
guess that's why I keep with poems
and no sleep and back aches
'cuz when I do slow down
from waking up,
and feel kind fingers knead that spot
just above my tailbone I know
that is right —

that I can live buckets of lives
without seeing faces glow
or smolder over my poems,
yeah, *that* is why it continues
and nothing belongs to me.

Stupid, I

had a sudden fear I'd be inadequate for you someday
since you wrote me a poem and it was truly good —
not "good" because it was for me, I'm just afraid
to let you down, to have wasted your ink,
though I'd think you'd be happy
having nonetheless written a work
that captured me on a shoreline somewhere
as you scribbled that green carpet down —
I just fretted a new edition to what would surely become
another pile of me arguing me. I hope you keep
your poem for me, it is heart and sweet and the only one
about just me unless you count the time
my sister wrote how my soul is like
a treasure chest — she didn't know me then,
we were children, and sadly,
now she wouldn't consider a rewrite
since she talks me up at parties
in Atlanta while quietly misunderstanding my work
and hiding my gay and plotting with mother
to find what little boy there is left
and dig inside for remnants of 18-carat dust.

Reach over, on the other side of this comma,
there are a few pieces of paper left
on which I'd like a copy of the best words
ever kissed in my direction —
don't go thinking your poem about me
is terrible because I love it so.

Informative Television

News anchor said we wouldn't find the bombs.

I said mother,
why do you watch the news
so early in the morning? How can you?

I work all day,
nine to six, I can't watch it there.

I said,
you don't have to watch anything
anywhere,
you want that chaos in your head
to carry around all day, stories of death
and anger and accusation?

Sometimes I need to see
who it is I have to pray for.

I said, pray for yourself.
We're just bullies,
not getting anything done.

Please, son, don't say something like that
when Miss Dot comes down the way,
she has a son-in-law in the war.

I said,
don't you see,
we can't find the bombs,
everyone's dead and there are no bombs,
we've stolen their lunch money,
there are no bombs,
why don't you
watch tornado footage on Channel Three?
There are no bombs.

She sipped coffee and said   *Your poems*

aren't good, I read what you leave around.

So I wrote a shit poem I may frame
for Mother's Day, send it to her and the last
son-of-a-bitch who said my poetry was bad.
Of course it is.

But he probably watches the news, too,
looking for bombs he's stupid enough
to believe will save us,
lurking like an asshole.

Just like an asshole.

After Dreaming of My Hands

Looked at my hands this morning
and never felt so aware of how they work
being dry, damaged,

my left index finger shredded
by multiple beer bottle caps —
Nathan would hate my hands
since they don't grip a pew's edge,
and I don't have steady knees
that routinely genuflect,
he hates me,
   not brave enough to say it
he's the worst, with opinions stopping
just before they join the world
through his spit scowl —
just say it, coward —
I told him he wasn't improving in poetry
and thought long, hard how being dishonest
is a cheap way to call God a savior.
I've sworn to do that
but
I don't feel like rebelling
against myself today,
it's beautiful, mid-morning,
a writer friend is on her way
to drive me out in it,

perhaps I should mention war
somewhere in here, make this about conflict
and give it to Nathan.
I still don't feel well,
which doesn't make me stop thinking
but I can't think quick, left the faucet running
in the bathroom — mother teased —
I changed a bulb for her — we all know how I feel
about mother, and now Nathan,

if you're reading this,

I like my hands.

Third Place Loser

She's mad, and I'd hold her hand
but it's a claw —
John knows,
Carol knows,
Belle knows as Belle works
making Belle drinks

that it was hot for all that poetry —
coffee shops should serve alcohol
to tame her feeling the angriness at night,
animosity loud inside her.
She's trying to get it out, and again,
I should hold her,
shake out those blank stares
all that silly slippery stinky verse
birthed on Friday.

I needed wine, promised to drink it
like heroin — this gorgeous boy
read about his grandmother.
Mine is dead.
I'd like to make love to him
but he's too driven, academic
(English, Theology)
or maybe just screw
after he leaves the seminary.

No matter,
my "she" liking murder and all,
that curly boy,
not sexy,
so sweaty,
she would punch a child
for loud bad energy,
like a soccer ball
she said she wanted to kick it,
kick it *so* down.

It's funny, truly,
people still get mad about poems,
but seriously
all it amounts to is $15.00 prize money
and me sticking my friend's pen in my nose
somewhere in a bar
and not in a poem.

Title for Sunday

We haven't yet written of love,
don't know if we should,
don't know much past not knowing,

don't know if we'd buy a cat
to suffocate the numbness,
or to write about when we're fresh out of poems
on waves, drifting ducks, being uninvited,
tension felt when we scribble revolution down

like you said

you couldn't write out
but you do, in green,
an awkward green still legible after frustration marks
and distracting sighs that don't stump me like they stump you —
I'd like to smoke another Camel
to scare cyclist couples from nosing over your shoulder
as if the wind wasn't enough —
and thanks for the Bukowski book —
    I wait for Christmas, like the rest,
for underwear and cheap cologne,

but my grandmother's gone, so no more ties.

To the Girl on the Edge of the Couch

Thanks for waking me this morning —
Sue said that poem
on how stupid my mother is
was a good poem last night,
and then we started drinking,
more than before we met with Sue.
Now it's close to noon
and my belly is creeping over
the end of starvation.
I had an erection
when you sat at my side
wondering why I didn't sleep
with a blanket,
pillow on my crotch,
and you read Millay
which was a nice way
to start the day.

And I appreciate you dreaming
about me last night —
I'll bet I snored across the house,
waiting for this moment
to arrive when we'd, for once,
wake up before nightfall,
not think about cigarettes
but writing letters,
hangover poems,
Gran bleating about
like a goat,
if goats are the ones that bleat,
and I'm trying hard
to mention somewhere
how you shaved my head
last night,
and so there it is,
my promised poem for waking up
on the right side of everything.

Trying to

hold on tight
to the light control of lamps—
only two work in this office,
but the music's good
and I feel like I'm on the road
tonight, not sitting here
watching dim shades of something I used to be
trickle down beside gnats and flies
that think about voice,
or Muse,
once part of a three-way with inspiration,
a tyrant who looked much like myself
and an uncomfortably green monkey
me and my woman carry around
when the beer is cold and the stars
afford us all a quiet drunk,

because I feel like a let down—
girl calls me nothing short of wrong
and I agree,
driveway cigarettes
don't bounce the right way for me
in the dark of Spring,
so cold in this house I forget
the state I'm in,
what state I'm in,
the streets are calling
with guitar and drumming dashboards,
my fingers cook on a different
surface that feels like a keyboard,
I feel my bed again, a song
clasping my ears the same way
a former lover said *Marbs*,
force me, don't push
and I thought he fucked in fiction,
lived in poetry without knowing how
we've come too far to lose,
too short to win—

being under thirty is being incognito,
don't we all think? I'd love to ask
anyone but the bare-faced cartoon
that looks away from the computer screen,
counting the minutes,
thinking about backpacks and assuming,
for the last time, that love means shit
past curiosity —
I called my best friend a chocolate bar a while ago
before we switched philosophy,
told her how we get mad and mad
when those little plumber words
don't leak out the right way
and we try to eliminate stanzas,
brood, disregard what's beyond the poem
other than the shag carpet beneath my toes,
rings on hers, the best way I could think her a mural
of wonderful,
a nice walk down bayside avenues
where old people fall
before they know they're old

and very varicose, I miss my boy
but don't love him the way my girl's
real eyes believe in me when I wake
from the couch and wipe my lashes,
sandals flapping like a mid-morning lecture
on harmony and finding the floor —

a cold beer is on my throat
like a raw oyster, just one,
I'll put the long,
long plural in a better place
like gas station ghetto cocktail grape
and having that impeccably timed hand
of hers on my neck,
like a suggestion, being the only real thing
I write about when I'm not wrapped busy
in a chokehold, wrestling my drunk fucking self
into the trash with the rest of my poems.

Twenty Dollars

was the title of an old poem
I wrote in a cow town
two and a half hours North
of the Gulf of Mexico,
depending on who is driving.

The poem meant nothing,
mentioned twenty students
in the classroom,
one breathtaking, quiet boy
named Curtis,
I suppose I equated
them all with money for metaphor —
upstairs, a professor thought
the piece great and I
threw it in the trash.

The real twenty dollars
is, right now, on the coffee table
lying next to a dime
plucked from the driveway
this afternoon. For my friends,
it's the same million bucks
it is to me, like an envelope
from Mike in bow-tie
sending a personal check,
handwritten letters
from NYC, all saying,
relax, you are compelling,
have a drink on me

and this jobless afternoon,
hours before I go on
at this swank martini lounge
and close down the reading
of poetry behind a Pulitzer-prize nominee
I realize, Mike sent that money
so I can be free,

can enjoy that difficult folded bill
that can't get me too much,
a few beers for friends, a generous tip,
maybe comfort somewhere
in knowing he thinks me good,
better than the Pulitzer,
worth more than wasting
titles on dead poetry,
balling it into garbage,
unlike how I handle
that twenty,
diffidently crisp,
folded with innocent glee
in the poor, happy shadow
of my left pocket.

On Feeling Unhealthy

It never fails, one gets older
and realizes as children
we bounced back so nicely
from everything. I sit in green
and this is my voice today,
can't decide if I will smoke
tonight, very strange energies
of throat, the word *harsh* climbs in,
as well, though the bad breath
of all those horrible cigarettes
didn't stop that
not-so-diffident creature
from yelling to make love
with her harder —
she didn't really say it that way,
you know how it goes.

I feel unwell, right nostril
leaking,   left doesn't care
or hasn't paid close attention
and followed suit.   I was supposed
to watch my friend's house,
feed his animals, he didn't want
his lover to, but rather,
someone he could trust like me,
and I forgot, thinking if I were a kid
I would have remembered,
but when you drink so much
you find it easy to focus
on those environmental factors,
like colds, not a real panic
over some stupid yelping brown
mutt in a cage with no water
for a night,

and even at twenty-four I see nothing
boyish about me, and yes you can
say twenty-four isn't old but sirs

and ma'ams, I'm probably older
than you, with man-ankles,
hairy hair, nothing smooth
or eclectic-sexual about this vessel
any longer, and it will get worse,
which is fine, too — who stands to meet me
will have to love me
and nothing else —
snot-nosed or not,
I was as a child,
someone still cared.

We Said Puppies

Last night John's *yes*
was strong in his hands —
I think sign language
works like his fingers
did and do,

I suppose

we write honest enough,
so loud and hear thoughts
like voices over our shoulders
and damn, by the way,
Sue was blank
looking for us, our wisterias,
she loves Dickey, Collins,
we know   and wonder if there's
a sign for loving writers —

you go ask John
and
thanks for that,
your whisper —

it echoes when you think
it doesn't —

it does —

we both
laughed while junkie Pam
cleaned that beer I kicked over,
funny how the beer
wasn't mine   never is
or the mop you brought to clean
beneath my feet —
I remained couched
and so
there has to be a way
to sign "lazy" —

you go ask John.

Accidentally Written on the 9th of October

Haven't written you a poem in a while.

Such a powerful word, lady, how you
write a great letter, say things like
"discordant" when I least expect,
know you don't mean what you say
when you say, when you let words drip,
drop because you are able, *do* return,
whisper things like John's bedewed haiku
in my ear and apologize for simplicity
so I can laugh and say I foresaw it
and you can grin and I can wonder about you,

why I haven't written for so long,
maybe that I was afraid of you,
your connotations, having made love
to your denotations by verse,
by second chances to scribble love poems
and call them poems because that darling boy
who may or may not have bought me flowers
said it drove him crazy since I call *you*
my favorite poem on the road, in red circles,
straight circles, away with me,
remember (?) the piano around that expression,
the pain you said involved you
in missing me, that it ached (in the night)
to the point you forgot splendor,
recalled chance, told me *yes* against the cold

in the couplets I'd forgotten to send you,
ones you said would break you if all
I were to do was whisper Ophelia from the water,
you, write you one more line in the dark,
the heated, repeated nuisance of dark

that I'd die if you would simply come.

Advice from a Voice

Afraid to let the computer rest,
my friend, so late in the evening,
my hand is sore from thinking,
eyes from dreaming — all right —

I was planning a run until I went to power off,
tried to push myself into shoes
unlock the front door
greet the chill with two shirts
exercise pants
stretch my elbows
seek victory in the streets
I've had a sandwich and a hug today,
ready to run like a short opera,
fueled by remembering
a gorgeous young man
so beautiful I feel alone, you see,
it is impossible to run when my brain
has prepared all but my heart

(I will need it to make it back)

so move away from the keys
you should tell me
try so hard not to think
I can hear you now

your poem will find you
on a midnight-stained cul-de-sac
circling and circling,
waiting to be carried home

Any

Wrote a story in my head last night—
characters drafted through a nightmare
wedged against the corner of the bed,
had it lined in poetry, edited by dawn,
prepared for publication between the sheets
and snored it senseless through derision,
melancholic rebuttal at the rain
fell mindlessly by the windows,
open windows of the bedroom—

woke to the sound of cold, and *and*,
unneeded *ands*, unwanted ands
pounding the roofs and ceilings,
the stone beside the door, my bare feet
running carpet down in furled, unfurled
shifts, a breakfast boy on his errands,
the story of course lost outside of me,
having fallen from my loose pockets
as I poured from bed still clad
in battle gear, having had whirled sticks
and fire near the grave of sleep, opium
on my lips, the music of a boy
that terrible woman in even my best of dreams
was supposed to hate me for,
time I left myself alone long enough
to know she'd hate me in the morning,
any mourning, and that stories of any worth
would never, not a chance in the hell of day,
bring me peace, not ever, like her love,
any love, her kind (I've said before)
has broken me, painfully, a silence
intolerably searing, a cruel sort of broken
over which Muriel would strangle her to dust,
so save me, please, before I've mastered
the craft of losing heart.

Wednesday Work After Oversleeping

Got Bonnie in my head
'bout making me an angel,
don't feel like flying, though—

had this woman to my left
with big blue eyes and dry,
red-orange hair
across the blinking blues,
told me about a mission
and interrupted me about Israelis
and Palestine and war
and fences
and lists of things she wanted
to avoid like fences, lists,
demonizing people—

I told her she wasn't
in the slightest, she said
"thanks for telling me that"
and interrupted me again
about "the Father,"
that she didn't care
about repercussions
when it came down
to the Lowered Gawd All-Matty
and she shook my hand,
hers was small and fat
(the kind of small and fat
you expect from a woman
who tells you she may or may not
be an orphan or an angel)—

my hand was warm and rigid—

she walked the hall
very slowly and far away
in all denim,
thinking she may have converted me

by simple handshake
and I thought,
not in that outfit, honey,

and I watched until she was gone
and I skipped across the hall,
hummed about that *old rodeo*
and thought how long it's been
since I passed through Montgomery.

Two Cents

I wrote my number on back
of an adhesive strip and the boy asked
my name, although ours is the same,
and then he laughed, said "of course
I can remember…who *else's* number
do I have on a Band-Aid"

and I wonder, now, drinking beer
in my office with Dylan on the player,
contemplating another six-pack
down the street or hashing out
another pre-drunk poem before they get
really bad and lower my own (bar)
for easy access, Christ,
the kid was so attractive, I should have
kissed him when he asked if I was gay

but I didn't, thinking that when you call me
from Boston by midnight, I'd rather have
nothing to tell you for once, hear you out
a bit, let your drunken smile
slip into the phone and close down my day,
same way my stories do you when you have
nothing to say, or when you secretly hold back,
and I bet there were times you did.

Puzzled

Trying to discern whether now or always
is usable in poetry since now constantly ends
and always never arrives,
never say never is a cliché, too,
like hope in tomorrow,
tomorrow never (there it is again)
all right *only* gets you closer to always
which seems infinite

but we're raised
and taught that nothing lasts forever,
to hope for everything
and expect that which lasts forever,
so I suppose that if I write now in a poem
it is for the exact moment
I sit and put down an idea, feeling,
etc., knowing that nothing will come of it,
the moment will pass into a different series
of nows and a few thens
before the poem is put to bed and that,
I believe, will always have
the comfortable tendency
to mean everything to me.

If This

Quietly she's bright by love,
and if I knew that it meant she'd publish
in the Paris Review and everyone
would love her work,
do/line/breaks/when/they/broke/her/apart
in an analytical paragraph
I'd have first broken her heart
and played Yorn records
until no one wanted to try to say
she needed dimming, way she loved so hard
in the northern cold the world needed to see

and/still/she's/so/very/well-lit

even when I tell her I lost that poem
ignored by New Orleans and California
and Iowa and New York,
the confession of faith I mentioned
in a letter to my sister,
about my *other* her I was so caught I thought
she'd be enlivened by the words on the page,
and I bet she was
for a moment

spread out against her will
like that professor who nodded at her blue light,
said she hadn't anything on the cold
she burned so warm/I/wondered

if I could beat a drum to her step,
would it again catch the poem,
blanked out in the dark that night
the music was as hot as red wine
and I called her, said,
I lost a bit of you I never guaranteed
and then drank more wine without her
like I haven't her now,
thought she'd come all this way to say in a day

that we'd never make it,
such life getting in the way
I tell you, reader,

if/this/is/making/sense
you, too, have loved.

Classical Poem Without *the*

A Beethoven sonata just ended —
I've been awake barely ten minutes
but time enough to eat an apple,
have a glass of water,
think how I will step outside
(sun is bright)
and lace my shoes for another fine walk —
I do hope birds are out.

Need to shave and work on my novel
today and tomorrow but cannot
quite get violins from my head
nor image of Ludwig on ground
ear to floor
to "hear" his compositions —

it would make me sad if I didn't already know
that one has to be a little crazy to create beauty
which is why I'm fairly normal
sitting at computer screen spilling thoughts
so recklessly about office
in pajama pants and not on floor

there is nothing to "hear" in my work
only ideas and me saying to all *I'm sorry,*
just want to be a little crazy too.

Figuring

I wrote you a poem
about twenty dollars,
and now, one considering
the hundred you sent
because you know I'm
moving to Illinois and
I've a novel on the way
how daft of me to think
you'd have the time
to read it in its entirety
on a cold day in December,
do you remember that it
was my birthday on the 4th
when I asked you to take time
to say, Marbs, I know you
didn't write this,
there must have been
a softer side, so I could say,
in a new letter, Mike,
you are too right, a nicer guy
than myself wrote this book,
and he dasn't call it a novel,
yes, I decided a man should,
at least once, say the word
dasn't and mean it.

First Poem Since Then

It feels right, the way I think
how you-not-here has caused
me to stop writing, how I cannot say
I bought a Monk collection
to your lips, watch them light up
like when you tell me about 'Trane
or footsteps in the snow,
ice formed over layers of Miles
between us, my bare black knuckles
on Sleep's wistful trumpet,
it feels wrong to tell you
that I can't create
that I can't sleep
that I can't hold you pressed
    to my ear, listen to you excite
    over nights out with girls
    and tenor saxophones
that I can't say to you by mail
    those maddening sounds of lonely
    which wrench my back
        nightmare after nightmare
that I can't let you let me be me
that I can't be free on a highway
    other than the one
    leading to you, I should say
that, I should tell you
    I am only alive

because

it feels right, the way I know
how you-somewhere-else
feels wrong, as me-not-there
is our foulest unfairness,
life and love
are not through,

not yet,

128

there is more Chet Baker
and more unfound roads for lovers
to litter with our poems,
the ashes I've become
since we cried ourselves apart
in that Illinois mourning wind.

To Muriel

Write a poem,
sweetheart,
in your head
and dancing fingers,

ballad me nightly,

sonnet my bedroom
with your eagerness,

fill me with an ode —

go write a poem
and do not make it fast,
I'll guard your wine
as you scribble
and spill,

sestina me into the grave,
please,
write a poem —

elegy me into the morning
that I might wake
to kiss your nose,
tears still fresh
like an undead dream.

Wannabes

She seeks open road,
paints canvas to play out
the silence beneath our poems,
verses versus us
and vice versa —
she giggles
about a good song,
an elephant
from the paneled walls
around her rocking chair,
I think she's crazy a bit
loudly, she asks me to come look,
come see how she is poem-ing
alone with her laughter
of which I am jealous
and equally glad that music
pours from our ears
without sound,
she just chuckled the word
"betwixt,"
I'd think we're in danger of something,
a friend says they should be longer,
all of them, the poems tonight
about her own *un*likelihood
and she'll feel need
for vituperation,
of this I am prescient,
we have spent too many nights
with a dictionary
like sober literati
and less to ourselves (I consider)
in the quiet betwixt her laughs,
my sickly sinuses
and the wheezing of the fan
pushing us both
around pretentious corners
one dusty bookshelf
at a time.

Dictum

We saw real grass today.
First time in two months our shoes
met what lurked beneath the snow.
It took two days of sun — "they" said
it was a milder winter than usual.
You stepped in mud
and called it mud.

I didn't imagine then
I'd be holding your hand
in the car, leaving the liquor store,
tears down your face,
hating to cry the way
you hate to cry,
just those trivial hours between sadness
and the outside lawn. Who would
have thought it,
either you or me? I bought you cigarettes
so I can smoke them.

Thing is,
I can't shake this day or the rest I owe
these poems, rattling, shaking inside
while you are in the bedroom past midnight,
not having sex or writing poetry on your own.
If there are still tears,
I think the pinot grigio has grown colder
in your absence, remembering that
all the day was meant to be
was us marveling at how, pretty soon,
there will be no more snow fights,
no more scraping of the windshield,
maybe a few more stained cheeks
and then no more us.

What I Did, I

fixed a new drink
and read the rest of you,
your fingers clack-clacking
in the back room in which I will live
once we buy my new bed next week
and I can then lapse into the hermitage
we discussed four months ago.

I will only become less lively
as this winter wears on.

But your new work is marvelous,
an extreme sort of marvelous
that will keep you sleepless
most nights, and then you will
be like me, hanging from the eaves
so that the bite of the wolf
cannot find your frightened heels,
looking down at the demons
looking up
I know
this is going to be the beginning
of the end for you and,
when the end is over,
I will be rigid at the finish line,
drink in hand,
barefoot and timid wearing a t-shirt
that says *start*,

holding a towel that reads
I told you so.

Tonight, Well Shaken

About his daughter who died:

That was the poem you mentioned,
pasted in some old scrapbook of yours
I used for an ashtray.

The translation from French was below it.

Wind pressed inward the folded blinds
from agape windows behind us.
I told you to write a poem.
I knew you would.
You'd already done it.
You can do it on cue.

You can read from *A Farewell to Arms*
and get out of your head with me.
That is how it's to be.

We agreed martini glasses make a home.
I threw one at you. It broke nicely.
We'll have to buy more,
all this passion walking about the house.

At least the drinks were good
while they lasted, while they were cold.
While they contributed to the goodness of night,
the same night from a page turn
in our ashtray of your memories,
the cut-out where Ernest said
night can be for lonely people.
It will kill them.

We know it will.
The glass will fly.

We will take to wings,
float a bit together before our goodbyes,

before writing poems for the dead.
Poems we hope will make sense of it all.

They will. Believe me.
But only when we're courageous enough
to discern what sense might be.

For a Girl Who Doesn't Sleep

I've got one quick page
to give you assurance
that we'll get stoned tonight
and write more poems
maybe
watch that movie
with men discussing
The Iliad in a bar
and then drive headlong into night
        I've got just
one short stanza
to tell you
a poem's not a poem
unless it comes from
fast truth,
        that child you hide
like
        a demon you can't pacify
each night you climb in bed
and you can't do it
alone.

5:33 A.M., April

This night has become a strange,
twisted thing,
with New York men
and aspirations for velvet,
loving jazz and loving me
or loving jazz to become more of me
like jazz,
brooding, thumping,
fingertip-dancing in the brain,
these queers that stumble,
rootless,
tsunamis in my aorta unfounded
and insane —
I hate what the dark has become,
an unlived memory that beckons itself,
haunting, effortless,
music no human can sing.

Interesting Thing About Neighbors

A geologist is staring through her
kitchen window
from across the street
at me smoking underneath
our torn
ragged American flag
that still hangs despite
the weather
I would guess
she finds my process interesting
how I stand on the porch and watch the night
and listen to my roommate
scream across the house
that she can hear me packing smokes
to the beat of a Miles Davis track
and
even though she doesn't know Miles
like I know Miles
she still calls out in the dark
from her bed
as the geologist folds back the blinds
and lets out her Labradors
to bark at me for knowing something
they sure as hell don't.

That Highway Between What I Would Tell Her

Under ferns we talked into a late night.
       We spoke of some wild talk of business
like Matt knew I knew business
he did
he knew I knew business
under the ferns
where nothing wavered
like apologies
or cigarettes
or things left unmentioned
this old way of writing poems
across a porch we've sat before
he said he
scared someone into submission
and then put out his smoke —

I've figured we've done our best
in this house
to remember on our own
how we used to be,

Matt being apart from me,

(and some used to think him gay
because he's so gentle
and kind
but
if that makes a fag
I'm counted out)

under ferns,
the ferns that sway when they will
with ice-cold fingertips
just begging to have someone
touch them
without punctuation
just touching them alone.

You Want Me To Write About Conflict?

I spend all this time
writing poetry
if that's what you'll call it
     one day
when I am dead
and this is what remains
know I write it for myself
for when it gets warmer
and the audience warms to poetry
     I can't imagine why anyone would think
a poet's life is worth admiring
     I guess it's about longing
and jealousy
all wrapped in a ball
since everything gets wrapped in a ball
these days
as you sit at the computer
like I do
hating the computer
and the drink
just to say a few words of nonsense
as though maybe
just maybe
I could reach another human being
when it's cold
but not really
not really cold
like this warm
young
dumb wealth of tragedy
that will get me nowhere
when I put down my fingers
and think that this is the answer
all this waiting by the phone
for someone to ring
and say
I've read your work
You're amazing.

Joe

I gave you smokes
as you drew down the blinds
when I was writing poems in my sleep
over cold coffee while Amber
bled her brains awake
across the table
and so I think it should be said
I liked shaking your hand most
out of all those lovely people
who said life was perfect
this morning
because I never believed them
since they weren't you and never will be
brother
they will never be as pure as you.

Frank Passed By

That yellow flower
wasn't his to give,
he'd simply plucked it
from a gate down Bradford Street
and still
he gave it to me
as I stepped from my car
and stretched a tired stretch
into the gray air overhead.
I think
he gave it because I needed
to be reminded
that in every instance there
is something far more beautiful
than the beauty you're
experiencing,
it's just that
we sometimes forget to check
and see
same as admiring a pretty envelope
without realizing there's money
inside
which is not
to say that Frank's flower
is as worthless as money
but rather
a guarantee that hope is
nothing more than a little
yellow petal
in your outstretched palm.

Old Man in the Diner

If I were a fisherman
I'd walk a morning harbor
and discuss my dreams
with a deckhand
and maybe talk of knots
or triggerfish throats
before the sun hit the water
and my life swam away
with the waves.

What Love Means To Me, So Young

Belly getting pregnant from brownies —
Muriel yacks through the door
from there to poetry,
compliments me on the icing
job I pulled, licked some off my finger

and she did that cute forward bend
like she wanted to take the spreading knife
in her mouth from my hand —
I said something about going down
and called it a vagina knife.

She didn't pay much attention,
sees me as a human rhetorical question
with no punctuation, or like a guy
who needs help with his hair
growing out too fast in the back —
she offered to shave it twice
this afternoon when we didn't know
she'd be cooking and writing
her best poems ever
around the house while I sat in the hot seat,
in front of this damn computer
and drank steamy coffee,
griped about being sweaty
in the South in mid-April,
and she said shut your mouth
so I did —
it was amusing
when she interrupted
to give me a pinch of hot brownie
and a milk-sip —
she told me it could have stood
by itself without the icing.
I reacted fast,
said shut your mouth,
too —

Muriel scratched the back
of my head and smiled,
whispering,
Marbs, you just don't know.

Acknowledgements

This collection of poems is for...

Paige Coker (fellow cave-dweller), Dr. Sue B. Walker (taught me to write at all times and costs), A. Meagan Davis (for sharing the sunrise), all women of talent and light and *incredible* patience. I admire you and thank you, thank you, thank you.

My mother, Beverly, for her championship and seeing integrity in me amidst all the noise.

My sister, Lindsey Marbut-Kallos, for being my steady and true mentor, as well as my partner in catching lightning bugs in mason jars, way back when.

Michael F. Shugrue, my first hero of adulthood and to whom my debut novel was dedicated. The word "wonderful" will always be yours.

Photographer Larry Graham, (www.grahamstudioone.com), for a connection through art in our incomparable French Quarter community.

My editor, Peter Jelen, an artist and writer who acts more as my optometrist than an editor, helping me see the world more clearly.

My husband, Michael Quintana. For reminding me to breathe, I love you first and before all of this.

And Muriel. Vision. Fist of blue punching the ether. Or maybe not. Maybe better. Sipping tea, rightly, miles away and telling your perfect story.

About the Author:

Damon Ferrell Marbut lives in New Orleans, Louisiana. His works have appeared in *Garbanzo Literary Journal*, *The Conscious Reader*, *Literary Kicks* and *Brevity Poetry Review*, among others. He has published several articles on modern publishing, including with *The Penmen Review* and *Southern Writers Magazine*. His debut is the acclaimed coming-of-age novel, *Awake in the Mad World*.

GrahamStudioOne

© Larry Graham

Also available from
BareBackPress

Better Than God
Peter Jelen

ONLY HUMANS CAN BE HUMANE

Michael's father is steadily deteriorating from Alzheimer's. In his rare moments of lucidity, he begs for death. As much as Michael wants to believe that his father's pleas are part of the disease, he knows in his heart, that they are a suffering man's last wish. How can Michael help his father die ~ peacefully?

Better Than God is a collection of dark and humorous fast paced, imaginative stories, like Menting, Survival of the Swiftest, and Confining the Critic.

$18.99
ISBN 13: 978-0988075016
254 Pages
BIASC: Short Stories

Celebrating Death
Shannon Lyndsy

ENVIRONMENTALISM IS SPREADING ACROSS THE WORLD LIKE FACEBOOK. MORE AND MORE PEOPLE ARE GOING GREEN, AND NOT JUST FOR THE SEX.

It's the beginning of the end of the world and Sean Logan thinks he has the power to stop it. As a member of Generation Z, a group of HIV positive environmentalists who have willfully contracted the disease in order to depopulate the planet and save Earth from further human harm, Sean crusades to convert as many people as possible, spreading the cure, and preaching the message of Generation Z ~ for the greater good.

$18.99
ISBN 13: 978-0988075030
244 Pages
BISAC: Fiction

Unwrapped:
The BareBack Anthology

Unwrapped: The BareBack Anthology is a collection of innovative poetry from poets speckled around the world who have been featured in BareBack Magazine, an online publication dedicated to BareBack writers. People who aren't afraid to take off their gloves and give the world sincere, unpretentious, honest writing that has punch.

$17.99
ISBN 13: 978-0988075047
136 Pages
BISAC: Poetry

Old Gods for New
Mike Algera

At a sidewalk sale
you will meet a dealer
he will tell you
he has monuments of old gods
for sale, "Pick a God,
and worship however you please."

~ Excerpt from Old Gods for New

Old Gods for New reflects upon personal triumphs and demons, love and longing, the past and never-was; musings that spark both the artistry of playful banter as well as lyrical madness. Writing that is quirky yet daring, combining scratch words into something new.

$19.99
ISBN 13: 978-0988075075
138 Pages
BISAC: Poetry

www.barebackpress.com